D1711433

HIGH SCHOOL FOOTBALL

Robert Cooper

DiscoverRoo
An Imprint of Pop!
popbooksonline.com

abdobooks.com

Published by Pop!, a division of ABDO, PO Box 398166, Minneapolis, Minnesota 55439. Copyright © 2020 by POP, LLC. International copyrights reserved in all countries. No part of this book may be reproduced in any form without written permission from the publisher. Pop!™ is a trademark and logo of POP, LLC.

Printed in the United States of America, North Mankato, Minnesota.

052019
092019

THIS BOOK CONTAINS
RECYCLED MATERIALS

Cover Photo: Shutterstock Images
Interior Photos: Shutterstock Images, 1, 6, 7, 12, 14, 16 (bottom), 20, 28, 30, 31; Phelan M. Ebenhack/AP Images, 5, 19; Jacob Ford/Odessa American/AP Images, 8–9; iStockphoto, 11, 15, 16 (top), 22, 29; G. Newman Lowrance/AP Images, 13; Tammy Shriver/Times West Virginian/AP Images, 17 (top); Mike Janes/Four Seam Images/AP Images, 17 (bottom); Rob Roos/The Evening News/AP Images, 21; Red Line Editorial, 23; Kirby Lee/AP Images, 25; Morry Gash/AP Images, 26–27

Editor: Nick Rebman
Series Designer: Jake Nordby

Library of Congress Control Number: 2018964848
Publisher's Cataloging-in-Publication Data

Names: Cooper, Robert, author.
Title: High school football / by Robert Cooper.
Description: Minneapolis, Minnesota : Pop!, 2020 | Series: Football in America | Includes online resources and index.
Identifiers: ISBN 9781532163760 (lib. bdg.) | ISBN 9781644940495 (pbk.) | ISBN 9781532165207 (ebook)
Subjects: LCSH: Football--Juvenile literature. | American football--Juvenile literature. | High school football players--Juvenile literature. | High school athletes--Juvenile literature.
Classification: DDC 796.33262--dc23

WELCOME TO DiscoverRoo!

Pop open this book and you'll find QR codes loaded with information, so you can learn even more!

Scan this code* and others like it while you read, or visit the website below to make this book pop!

popbooksonline.com/high-school-football

*Scanning QR codes requires a web-enabled smart device with a QR code reader app and a camera.

TABLE OF CONTENTS

CHAPTER 1
FRIDAY NIGHT LIGHTS

Fall has arrived. High school football is about to begin. Students fill the stands to watch the first game. The players' parents are there too. They're ready to cheer their team to victory.

WATCH A VIDEO HERE!

High school football players in Florida compete in a game as fans watch from the stands.

A high school marching band prepares to take the field.

MANY ROLES

Students don't have to play football to get involved in the game. Some play in the marching band. Others are cheerleaders who pump up the crowd.

Most high schools in the United States have a football team. The

players are all students
at the school.
Family, friends,
and neighbors
gather on
Friday nights to
watch them play.

*A high school player
makes an impressive
catch during a Friday
night game.*

Schools in small towns may have

barely enough players to form a team.

Schools in big cities have thousands

of students. Their teams play in large

High school football players take the field as thousands of fans cheer them on.

stadiums. In some places, the games are

shown on local TV channels.

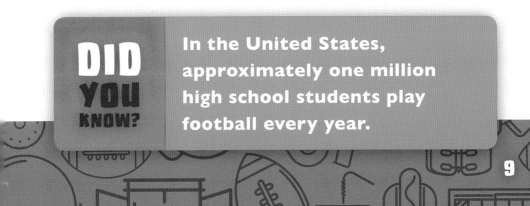

DID YOU KNOW?

In the United States, approximately one million high school students play football every year.

9

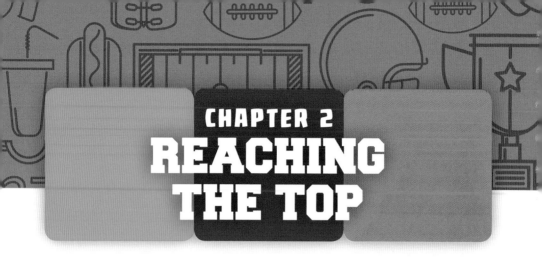

CHAPTER 2
REACHING
THE TOP

Most high school football teams start

practicing in August. Students must try

out for the team. Coaches watch the

students practice. They try to decide

which students are the best players.

The coaches select those students for

the **varsity** team.

Coaches work with players to help them develop their skills.

LEARN MORE HERE!

JV players can improve their tackling by practicing with dummies.

Many schools also have a junior

varsity (JV) team. The JV players aren't

as good as the varsity players. But they

build their skills. When JV players are

older, they may have the opportunity to

move up to the varsity team.

DID YOU KNOW?

Former pro quarterback Tim Tebow was homeschooled. But he played for the high school near his home.

Tim Tebow led the Denver Broncos to a playoff victory during the 2011 NFL season.

Players often run around cones to practice their quickness.

Some teams practice twice a day before the school year starts. During the school year, teams usually practice every weekday. The players also work on their skills outside of practice. They might watch videos of their games. Weight training is also common.

Lifting weights can help players build muscle.

TIMELINE

EARLY AUGUST

Teams begin preseason practices.

MID-AUGUST

The varsity team's players are selected.

LATE AUGUST

The regular season begins.

NOVEMBER OR DECEMBER

The **playoffs** begin.

NOVEMBER OR DECEMBER

State championships take place.

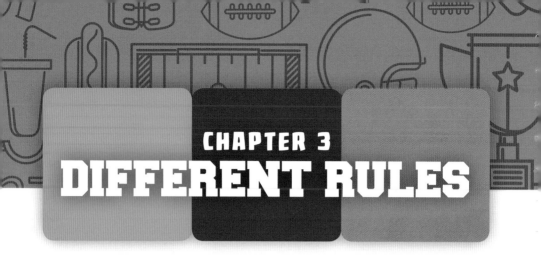

CHAPTER 3

DIFFERENT RULES

Most states put high schools into

divisions. The divisions are usually

based on how many students go to the

schools. Grouping schools by size helps

keep games fair. Big schools tend to have

LEARN MORE
HERE!

A high school team in Florida runs onto the field before the game.

more players. They also have more

money to spend on coaches.

A football team usually has 11 players

on the field at a time. But some schools

don't have enough players to make a

The running back is often one of the quickest players on the field.

High school players compete in an 8-on-8 game in Michigan.

full team. As a result, some divisions

use fewer players on the field. These

divisions might play 8-on-8 football.

High school football is very **popular** in Texas, California, Florida, and Georgia. These states have warm weather. That means players can practice outside all year. Many of the top players come from these states.

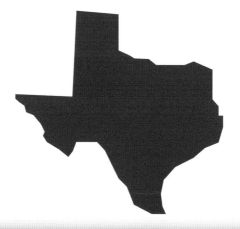

DID YOU KNOW? A high school stadium in Odessa, Texas, can hold more than 17,900 people.

STATES WITH THE MOST HIGH SCHOOL FOOTBALL PLAYERS

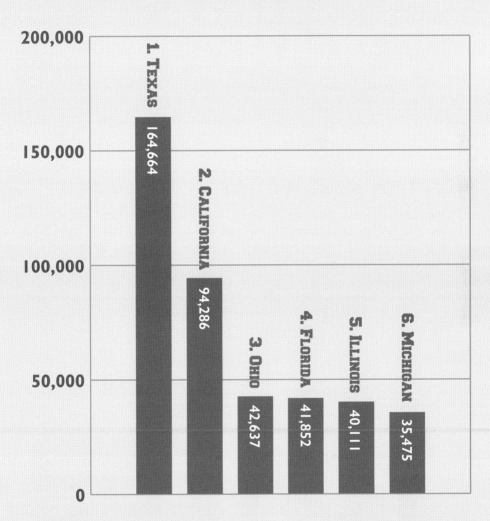

200,000

150,000

100,000

50,000

0

1. TEXAS — 164,664

2. CALIFORNIA — 94,286

3. OHIO — 42,637

4. FLORIDA — 41,852

5. ILLINOIS — 40,111

6. MICHIGAN — 35,475

*Accurate as of 2017

CHAPTER 4
STATE CHAMPIONS

Every team's goal is to win the state championship. To do that, a team must win lots of games during the regular season. After that, the team has to win every game in the **playoffs**.

COMPLETE AN ACTIVITY HERE!

A high school quarterback looks for a receiver during a 2018 playoff game in California.

The championship game usually happens at a **neutral** stadium. Each **division** has its own championship game. Some states hold the games at large college stadiums. High school players get a thrill out of using the same **facilities** as top college athletes.

DID YOU KNOW? More than 52,000 fans showed up to watch the Kentucky state championships in 2017.

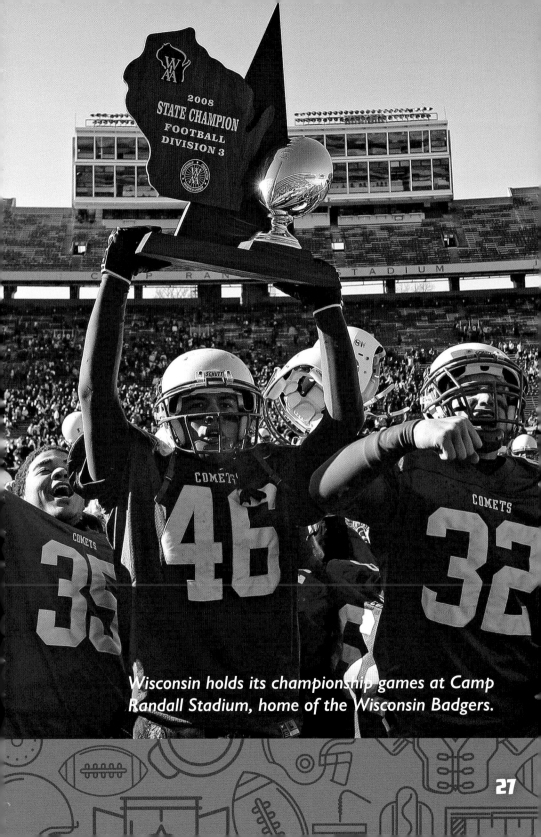

Wisconsin holds its championship games at Camp Randall Stadium, home of the Wisconsin Badgers.

27

High school football players often build strong friendships with their teammates.

The best high school players may go on to play football in college. But for most players, high school is the last time they will be on a football team. The students enjoy playing for their local community. Win or lose, they make memories that will last for years.

Playing under the bright lights is an exciting opportunity for many high school athletes.

MAKING CONNECTIONS

TEXT-TO-SELF

Would you want to watch or play high school football? Why or why not?

TEXT-TO-TEXT

Have you read a book about another sport that high school students can play? How is that sport different from football?

TEXT-TO-WORLD

Playing football helps high school students learn teamwork. How might this skill be helpful after high school ends?

GLOSSARY

division – a set of teams that play one another.

facility – a building that serves a specific purpose.

neutral – not home to either team.

playoffs – a set of games at the end of the season to decide the champion.

popular – liked by many people.

varsity – the highest level of a team at a school.

INDEX

ONLINE RESOURCES

popbooksonline.com

Scan this code* and others like it while you read, or visit the website below to make this book pop!

popbooksonline.com/high-school-football

*Scanning QR codes requires a web-enabled smart device with a QR code reader app and a camera.